Nina Lemon

Masking

Salamander Street

PLAYS

First published in 2024 by Salamander Street Ltd., a Wordville imprint. (info@salamanderstreetcom).

Masking© Nina Lemon, 2024

All rights reserved.

Cover design by Nina Lemon.

ISBN: 9781738429318

10 9 8 7 6 5 4 3 2 1

Further copies of this publication can be purchased from www.salamanderstreet.com

Wordville

Acknowledgements

Masking is an original play created with and for youth arts charity Peer Productions. I am especially grateful to my colleagues and trustees who helped bring this play to life. Movement Director Ruth Sparkes and Producer Alice Underwood deserve a special mention for the support and creativity they brought to the creation of the original production.

The following young actors were involved in research and development:

Ismael Akram, Eliana Barrs, Sophia Blanks,
Helen Blight, Alexa Botha, Seniha Ercan,
Poppy Hall, Alex 'Lexi' Harris, Olly Hembrow,
Jasmine Hill, Annabel Inskip, Imogen Lane,
Bella Leach, Katie Martin, Harry Meikle,
Alexandra Perry, Joe Phipps, Michael Seabrook,
Morgan Szarvas, Finchley Simpson, Archie Smith,
Bronwyn Teasdale, Nicole Williams
and Rhett Winwood.

Masking was originally performed on 20th February 2023 at Gosden House School before embarking on a tour of schools in the South East with the following cast and creative team:

Jamie:	**Harry Meikle**
Holly:	**Sophia Blanks and Poppy Hall**
Rosie:	**Eliana Barrs and Imogen Lane**
Alex:	**Michael Seabrook**
Nadia:	**Seniha Ercan**
Billy:	**Annabel Inskip and Finchley Simpson**
Dom:	**Rhett Winwood**
Director:	**Nina Lemon**
Movement Director:	**Ruth Sparkes**

DIRECTORS!
WELCOME TO *MASKING*:
A PLAY FOR YOUNG MINDS

If you're on the lookout for a compelling play that resonates with young performers and audiences alike, you've landed in the right place. I present for you *Masking*, a production born from the heart of my theatre company Peer Productions and crafted specifically for secondary schools in the UK in 2023.

Prepare to immerse your students and performers in the captivating narrative of *Masking*, a play that explores mental resilience, empathy and the profound impact of friendship. This versatile production offers the freedom of a simple stage setup while providing a canvas for boundless creativity and imagination.

The play's setting may be confined to a classroom, but the possibilities for expression and interpretation are vast and I want to empower all directors, teachers and performers working on *Masking* to explore the nuances of the script and to bring their unique visions to life.

An inclusive ensemble play

Featuring seven equally significant roles, each character falls within the age range of 13 to 17 and can be played by actors of any racial background. *Masking* offers three female roles, two male roles and two roles open to actors of any gender. Additionally, *Masking* includes two neurodivergent characters, providing a potential platform for neurodiverse performers to take the lead and contribute their unique perspectives. With a running time of around one hour, every character boasts a unique and a personal monologue, ensuring a plethora of opportunities for each performer to shine, making *Masking* an ideal choice for assessments or exams.

Although *Masking* tackles some hard hitting issues, there are no swear words in the text.

The play is originally set in a UK classroom, but you can easily adapt it to your local community. The play is about a generation whose formative years have been impacted by a global pandemic, so many of the issues will feel very familiar wherever you are. I've provided a helpful guide with specific references to make the transition smooth, creating a familiar and connected experience for both performers and audiences.

A play for young people about young people

I wrote the play working alongside young actors from my theatre company, and the text explores a range of issues that were important to them. Each character grapples with their individual mental health challenges. Holly battles an Instagram obsession, recognising its potential harm. Autistic Billy finds the change in routine overwhelming. Alex shoulders the responsibility of advocating for the LGBTQ+ community. Nadia is triggered to recall a distressing journey away from her home country, while Rosie fears for the dying planet. Jamie is plagued by anxiety, and Dom's concern for his sister Nancy adds a layer of tension. The play fearlessly tackles serious issues, offering young actors substantial dramatic material. Yet, it's not all shadows; interspersed with lighter moments and humour, *Masking* celebrates this often-misunderstood younger generation—a testament to their potential for compassion and care.

Two Worlds, One Play:

Masking seamlessly intertwines two realms—the locked-down geography classroom and the unspoken thoughts within each character's mind. This duality allows for diverse theatrical presentations, offering young actors a vast playground in which to hone their craft.

Classroom Dynamics: As the characters converse during this lockdown, the play provides opportunities for naturalistic exploration and the development of comedic timing, bringing the dynamics of their friendships to life.

<u>Internal Realms:</u> When delving into characters' unspoken thoughts, the language shifts into an expressive, poetic mode. In our initial staging, we emphasised this shift by incorporating a recorded voiceover alongside dynamic physical sequences, music and projection. Our production drew inspiration from the principles of Laban efforts, but feel free to explore other physical practices or draw inspiration from different practitioners and companies for your own unique interpretation.

However you choose to delineate these two worlds it's vital that the internal world stands out as markedly different from the present, underscoring a clear distinction between the two realms.

Make it your own

Each staging of *Masking* should be as distinctive as the young individuals and organisations behind it. I look forward to learning about your production experiences and hearing the responses from the young people involved.

Nina Lemon

ACTORS!
WELCOME TO *MASKING*:
A PLAY FOR YOUNG MINDS.

Are you set to perform in *Masking* or perhaps engaging in character work for your studies? Whether you're a seasoned actor with a string of performances or you're stepping onto the theatrical stage for the first time, I'm here to offer insights that will help you breathe life into the characters. It's my fervent desire that every rendition of *Masking* stands out as a distinctive and diverse creation, mirroring the uniqueness of the companies bringing them to life. Understand that my characters aren't solely mine as the playwright, nor do they exclusively belong to you as the actor. They reside in a dynamic space shared between playwright, actor and director, ensuring each interpretation becomes as distinctive as the creative minds shaping them.

Now, let's dive in with some simple questions and exercises to deepen your understanding of the characters.

Ask Questions

A proficient actor delves into the text, mining clues about their character. Utilise what the character says about themselves and what others say about them.

Inspired by the teachings of Uta Hagan, a German-born American actor and teacher, consider these nine questions:

1. **Who am I?** - Explore the character's name, age, physical traits, education and beliefs.

2. **What time is it?** - Delve into the era, season, day or even the specific minute.

3. **Where am I?** - Consider the country, town, neighbourhood or room.

4. **What surrounds me?** - Observe the weather, furnishings, landscape and people.

5. **What are the given circumstances?** - Examine what has happened, what is happening and what will happen.

6. **What are my relationships?** - Explore connections with characters in the play, outside the play or even inanimate objects or recent events.

7. **What do I want?** - Identify the character's desires in the moment or consider how these may change throughout the play.

8. **What is in my way?** - Uncover the obstacles the character must overcome.

9. **What do I do to get what I want?** - Explore the character's actions in pursuit of their desires.

Many of the answers to these questions can be found within the text. Let's explore Question 2, "What time is it?" as an example. While no specific time is explicitly stated in the play, several clues offer insights. The setting is a school, indicating a likely weekday between 8am and 4pm. In Scene 1, Nadia mentions having recently had lunch and, in Scene 14, Billy becomes distressed about potentially missing art club at 3:30 pm. Rosie expresses concern about picking up her little brother, and Dom contemplates his after-school Rugby practice. These hints place the play in the afternoon, likely close to 3:30 pm. Additional clues suggest the season may be Autumn or Winter; Rosie refers to the cold glass of the window in Scene 13, Billy opts for a hoodie and, in Scene 22, Jamie remarks on Nancy being "freezing up there."

Other questions may require a bit more imagination. Consider Question 6, "What are my relationships?" Take Rosie's character, for instance. The text provides substantial information about her connections. Rosie and Holly have been friends since primary school, with Rosie harbouring some jealousy towards Nadia, fearing she might be a better friend to Holly. Rosie also shares a connection with Alex, who checks in with her after she supports Nadia. Details about Rosie and Alex's relationship are limited so this is where your imagination can fill in the gaps. Rosie has a younger brother, and beyond this, nothing is known about her family. If you're portraying Rosie, consider building a broader picture of her family unit. Rosie's ability to provide mental health support to Nadia during a crisis also raises questions about how she developed these skills, adding layers to your portrayal.

Build a timeline or a lifeline

To better understand your character, use the text to build a timeline of significant events in their life. Depending on your character, there might be a wealth of information or just a little. For instance, Dom's final monologue shares key memories of his relationship with his sister over the years. On the other hand, if you're playing Holly, there may be fewer details available. We know she's been friends with Rosie since primary school and met Billy in year five. Nadia, however, is a recent addition to the school. If Holly found out about her ADHD through TikTok, it suggests a relatively recent diagnosis, given that it's unusual for a preteen to explore ADHD content on TikTok! Once your timeline has play-derived facts, you can fill in gaps by asking questions. For example, if you're portraying Alex, consider when the character came out to different people.

Improvise

To delve even deeper into your character, consider trying out improvisation for scenes not explicitly shown in the play. Here are some examples of scenarios to explore with your fellow actors, and feel free to invent scenarios of your own. If needed, other members of the cast can step in as different characters to assist in developing your character.

1. The day in Year 5 when Holly and Billy became friends.

2. When Billy first met new girl Jess.

3. When Alex came out to Dom.

4. Alex's conversation with his sister on the day he was chased to her flat by homophobic bullies.

5. Dom's efforts to engage his sister Nancy during a crisis.

6. Nadia's first day at the school.

7. Nadia comforting her father after having to leave their country.

8. When Rosie first became aware of the serious implications of climate change.

9. Jamie talking to a counsellor about exam anxiety.

10. Holly discussing with her parents about suspecting she may have ADHD.

Feel the freedom to experiment and let these improvisations spark new insights into your character's life and experiences.

Get Physical

Masking seamlessly blends two realms—the confined geography classroom under lockdown and the private thoughts of each character. It's vital that the internal world feels distinctly different from the everyday setting, emphasising a clear separation between the two spaces. One effective approach to explore this distinction is by employing a more physical theatrical style for the six inner world monologues.

Firstly, ensure that you and your fellow actors have ample space to move together and that the environment is free from potential trip hazards.

Do a basic physical warm-up to prevent muscle strain.

In our original production, we opted for recorded voiceovers for these monologues. While you may choose to perform them live, for this exercise, consider recording a preliminary version as a voiceover using your phone. This will allow you to focus solely on physicality at this stage.

You can explore the physical aspect with just the spoken text. However, if self-conscious, consider adding instrumental music with the right tone for the monologue. Don't overthink music choice; it can be changed later. Having some melody can guide your body movements.

Start individually. Play the voiceover track with your chosen music, observing how words and music prompt your body's movements.

Are there themes inspiring certain motions? For instance, in Jamie's monologue, he describes feeling frozen and stuck. How can you express this physical restriction?

After playing through the text with music individually, gather as a group to discuss ideas. How can individual movements contribute to a cohesive group sequence?

Identify any recurring physical motifs.

Consider the classroom setting. Incorporate objects or furniture that might be present. Ensure everyone is focused before incorporating objects, like chairs and tables. How can you safely manipulate these objects to transform the space and extend your movement?

Consider setting up a camera to watch back your improvisations and find moments for expansion or exploration.

Avoid extensive discussion; if needed, set a timer to limit group talk time between trying out physical ideas.

TRIGGER WARNINGS

- A character talking about exam stress, anxiety and panic attacks.

- A character talking about her love/hate relationship with social media.

- A queer male character talking about how homophobia and micro-aggressions impact his mental health.

- An Autistic character becoming overwhelmed and retreating into themselves and becoming non-verbal.

- A character who is a refugee experiencing flashbacks to her frightening journey away from her own country.

- A character experiencing eco-anxiety.

- A character becoming worried about their sister who has started to behave erratically.

- References to an off-stage character who, during a mental health crisis, has climbed onto the roof of a building at the school. The character is coaxed down off the roof by caring teachers and taken for help at the hospital.

- Extremely brief references to eating disorders, grief, OCD, personality disorders and learning disabilities.

MAKE IT LOCAL

Although the play is set in the UK, many of the themes will be resonant for young people all over the world. Feel free to adapt or change any specific references which don't make sense to the young people with whom you are producing the play. Here is a brief list of some specific words and references you might want to adapt with a brief explanation to help you on your way.

Page 1 - Holly says, "And, I swear to God, I nearly pooed my pants." I think only the British say pooed. Feel free to change this to pooped or something similar. I have deliberately chosen a childish and non-offensive word, so please feel free to find your equivalent!

Page 2 - The group talk about how Jamie as Deputy Head Prefect. A Head Prefect, sometimes called a headboy or headgirl is usually a high performing student who represents the school and contributes to the school's leadership. Often they are chosen by staff or elected by students.

Page 4 - A Curly Wurly and a Wispa are popular British chocolate bars.

Page 5 - In the UK students are externally examined in a wide range of subjects at age 16, and these exams are called GCSEs. GCSEs are now graded from one to nine with nine being the highest result you can achieve. Many students then focus on fewer subjects on which they are examined at 18, and these are called A-levels. During the Covid pandemic students in the UK did not attend school and external exams were cancelled.

Page 9 - Jamie refers to his mock tests. In the UK, students in exam years take practice papers internally, and these are referred to as mock exams.

Page 12 – Holly says, 'Maybe they've got an OFSTED inspection and just want us out of the way.' OFSTED is an organisation in the UK which inspects schools.

Page 13 and 24 - Dom refers to playing Rugby. Rugby is a contact team sport which is often associated with masculinity.

Page 15 - Channel 5 is a widely available TV channel in the UK. It is in part known for airing documentaries about unusual or embarrassing bodies.

Page 16 - Rosie is referring to the now Prince and Princess of Wales William and Kate and their daughter, Charlotte.

Page 18 - In the UK, it is common for people to greet each other by saying, "are you alright?" or simply, "you alright?" Often foreigners are baffled by this. If this doesn't ring true for your community change it to something that might be confusing to an outsider coming in to your area.

Page 19 - Rosie says, 'Some sixth former stalking a year 9 online.' In the UK children start school around age four in reception. They then enter year 1 and the years go up across settings numerically until they leave school in year 13. Years 12, and 13 are also referred to as the sixth form. Rosie is implying that it is inappropriate for Jamie, who is at least 17, so is over the legal age of consent, to be looking at 14-year-old Holly's social media accounts.

Page 24 - A rugby scrum is a set-piece formation that occurs during a rugby match and involves players from both teams coming together in a tight, organised formation.

Page 25 - Alex says, "Our teachers don't have to censor themselves for fear of promoting the acceptability of homosexuality." Here Alex is a alluding to Section 28, which was a legislative designation for a series of laws across Britain, that prohibited the "promotion of homosexuality" by local authorities. It was in effect from 1988 to 2003 in England. If this doesn't make sense for your setting, feel free to change the line or remove it completely.

Page 33 - Year 5 is the school year for eight and nine-year-olds.

Page 34 - When Billy refers to "Glinda, the good witch" they are talking about Glinda from the Wizard of Oz.

Page 38 - When Jamie refers to his EPQ he is referring to his Extended Project Qualification, which is an A-level standard, standalone qualification designed to extend and develop students' abilities, ready for university.

ABOUT THE PLAYWRIGHT

Nina Lemon is a playwright theatre maker and social entrepreneur from the UK. Back in 2006, she founded multi-award-winning theatre charity, Peer Productions, which specialises in peer education through theatre, training young actors to deliver new plays which tackle the issues which matter most to young people.

Nina's interests, as both an artist and an individual, lie in the furthering of human rights and she is particularly passionate about improving life changes for often marginalised groups including young people, disabled people and women and girls.

She is dedicated to developing new plays with and for young people and is currently researching a PhD exploring how plays can change the way young people think and behave in intimate relationships.

ABOUT PEER PRODUCTIONS

Peer Productions is an award-winning youth arts charity dedicated to transforming young lives through theatre. They do this through:

Training the next generation of actors and theatre-makers (aged 18 - 24 years) through our Peer Actor Development Programme (PAD) and Peer Employment Pathway Programme (PEP) for those with learning disabilities.

Touring our original plays to schools across the South East of England, performing engaging plays which support the National PSHE curriculum and tackle the issues that young people face in a compelling, compassionate and accessible way. These productions empower students to make positive life choices and to change the way they think about themselves and the world around them.

Projects in schools and in the community using theatre as a tool for social change.

Find out more - www.peerproductions.co.uk

CHARACTER BREAKDOWN

JAMIE - 17

Meet Jamie, a stellar student who finds joy in academic pursuits and excels in school. With an unwavering focus on education, Jamie's perfectionist tendencies drive them to place immense pressure on themselves to achieve success. Their commitment to academic excellence is evident in being chosen as Deputy Head Prefect, a role they relish for the added responsibility and influence it brings. However, Jamie struggles with expressing genuine emotions and tends to be judgmental of others.

Post-pandemic lockdowns, Jamie's world takes a turn as they grapple with panic attacks, particularly in the context of exams and studying, eventually leading to a diagnosis of anxiety. For Jamie, when they experience anxiety, they freeze and are unable to continue with what they are doing. This multifaceted character offers a rich exploration of academic prowess, perfectionism, anxiety and the challenges of emotional expression.

Jamie can be played by an actor of any gender or race. They/them is used but feel free to adopt pronouns that suit the performer.

BILLY - 14

Meet Billy, a 14-year-old with a diagnosis of Autism from childhood. For Billy, their Autism means that they sometimes can become sensorially overwhelmed in busy or noisy places. Plans and schedules are important to them, and they can struggle if too many plans change. Billy navigates mainstream schooling with additional support and doesn't face bullying. They possess a high level of empathy and are attuned to the moods and feelings of others. Friendships have deep roots, particularly with Holly, as they've been close friends since early childhood. They also love their dog Rudie.

Billy's role is open to actors of any gender or race, and they/them pronouns are used, though performers are encouraged to adopt pronouns that suit them. Ideally, the role suits a neurodivergent actor. In the original production, one actor portraying Billy also had a learning disability. Notably, Billy speaks less than other characters, choosing to communicate when they have something significant to express, making it an accessible role for those who may find extensive lines challenging.

HOLLY - 14

Meet Holly, a vibrant and chatty personality who has become a popular figure among her peers. Discovered to have ADHD a few years ago, this diagnosis has been instrumental in helping her understand herself better. For Holly, ADHD means she often blurts things out and can find it challenging to be organised and concentrate in class. However, her highly creative nature thrives in artistic endeavours, particularly excelling as a brilliant makeup artist with aspirations for a future career in the field. Holly loves social media. She is very kind and empathetic and is sensitive to injustices. In her social circle, Holly has been friends with Billy since childhood. Additionally, she and Rosie became best friends when they started secondary school two years ago, and her bond with Nadia has deepened over the last year.

Holly can be played by a female identifying actor of any race.

NADIA · 14

Meet Nadia, a 14-year-old who recently joined the school after moving to the country just a year ago. Her journey to a new land was prompted by the persecution her mother faced as a journalist back in their home country, where she wrote critically about the political regime. In our original production, the actor playing Nadia was Turkish, but the story intentionally allows for the character to come from various countries.

The abrupt departure from her homeland has left Nadia grappling with Post Traumatic Stress Disorder (PTSD), though it hasn't been formally diagnosed. For Nadia, her PTSD means she sometimes experiences nightmares. The stress within the play triggers a powerful flashback to the night she and her parents had to escape.

Since her arrival at the school, Nadia has formed a strong friendship with Holly. This connection provides her with a sense of support and belonging in her new environment.

Nadia can be played by a female identifying actor. Her race should be in keeping with decisions made by the director regarding the character's background.

ROSIE · 13

Meet Rosie, a thoughtful and intelligent young individual grappling with what some people now term eco-anxiety. For Rosie, her eco-anxiety translates into overwhelming worries and fears for the future of the planet. Consumed by these concerns, she dedicates considerable time to online research, finding it challenging to switch off from the looming specter of environmental disaster.

Rosie, driven by her convictions, has embraced a vegan diet and proudly identifies as an environmentalist. However, she is acutely aware that not everyone shares her concerns. This awareness sparks worry, especially in her close friendship with Holly, with whom she has built a strong bond. Rosie fears that her passionate commitment to environmental causes might be perceived as boring or alienating to her friends.

Rosie can be played by a female identifying actor of any race.

DOM - 13

Meet Dom, a 13-year-old brimming with excitement and playfulness, often seen as less mature than his peers, his exuberance shines in his love for being the centre of attention, always loud and lively. However, beneath this vibrant exterior lies a deep concern for his older sister, Nancy, who is sixteen. Dom senses that something is amiss but grapples with how to support her.

Nancy, yet to receive a formal diagnosis, is navigating some form of psychosis marked by rapidly shifting moods, erratic behaviour and increasing paranoia. Dom, despite his exuberance, harbours worries and uncertainties about his sister's well-being. His best friend is Alex, a connection that proves strong and meaningful despite their differences.

Notably, Dom is the only character without a monologue in the world of the unsaid. In the play's final scenes, a critical revelation occurs when Dom realises that his older sister, Nancy, is in crisis on the roof. This pivotal moment compels him to shed his playful facade, confront the reality of the situation and articulate his fears and frustrations aloud.

Dom can be played by a male identifying actor of any race.

ALEX - 14

Meet Alex, a quick-witted, bright, and humorous Gay 14-year-old. While his immediate family has been supportive, and his classmates accept him, Alex grapples with the nuanced impact of his sexuality on his mental health.

Despite the acceptance he experiences, Alex feels the weight of being seen as a representative for the entire LGBTQ community. The ongoing need to remain vigilant for his safety in the broader community places a mental toll on him. This continuous effort to navigate societal expectations can be mentally exhausting for Alex. Alex finds solace and support in his best friend, Dom, whom he cares about deeply. Their friendship provides a crucial anchor amidst the challenges Alex faces.

Alex can be played by a male identifying actor of any race.

Nina Lemon

Masking

SCENE 1

An alarm sounds. The students rush into the classroom and hide under their desks. JAMIE is the last to enter. They carefully shut and lock the door and take a deep breath. The alarm stops.

JAMIE: It's OK. Erm, you can come out. It's safe.

The students emerge.

HOLLY: Wow! That scared me. My heart's beating like crazy. (*To ROSIE*) Feel.

ROSIE sheepishly touches HOLLY's heart.

HOLLY: Can you feel that?

ROSIE: Yeah.

HOLLY: Huah. I'm still shaking

HOLLY reaches out for NADIA's hand.

HOLLY: And, I swear to God, I nearly pooed my pants.

ALEX: Charming.

ROSIE stops touching HOLLY's heart. HOLLY attempts to regain her composure fanning herself.

DOM: Alright. Calm down. It was obviously a false alarm.

ALEX: Or a test.

NADIA: A test for what?

ROSIE: Lockdown drill practice.

HOLLY: You know, if there's an intruder on site or...

BILLY: If there's been some kind of accident.

DOM: Or some madman's come in with a machine gun.

He jumps arounds pretending to shoot people

DOM: Babababababababababababa baba ba ba.

HOLLY and ALEX join in and act dramatically as though they have been shot.

NADIA: That's not funny.

HOLLY: *(Abruptly snapping out of it.)* Yeah, Dom you're so immature. *(To NADIA and ROSIE)* Come on.

HOLLY, NADIA and ROSIE start to try and leave.

JAMIE: I'm afraid you need to wait here.

BILLY: Why?

ROSIE: The alarm's stopped.

JAMIE: *(Awkwardly)* It's nothing to worry about but I've been asked by Mr Phipps just to stay in here with you folks and make sure you're safe while they deal with, erm... an incident with a pupil.

DOM: What?

BILLY: OK.

BILLY goes and sits down. They get out a book and start reading.

ROSIE: What sort of incident?

JAMIE: I can't really say...

ALEX: Why not?

JAMIE: It's just not really appropriate to discuss someone's private... I'm sure it will all be dealt with very quickly and then we can all be on our way. OK?

JAMIE sits at the teacher's desk and starts getting some homework out.

Pause.

NADIA: Are you a teacher?

DOM: As if?

NADIA: I dunno. I've never seen them before.

HOLLY: Yeah, you won't know because it was announced before you joined but we are in the presence of the one and only Head Prefect. Jamie Sinclair!

BILLY: (*Looking up from their book*) Deputy Head Prefect.

HOLLY: What?

BILLY: They're Deputy Head Prefect. Henrietta Smythe's Head Prefect.

DOM: Oooh, that's even worse.

ALEX: Something of a consolation prize.

DOM: You lost out to sweaty Hettie the yeti!

ALEX: Oh, the shame!

JAMIE: Don't call her that. She's a really nice girl and a very good friend of mine actually.

Some of the group make whooping noises.

ALEX: Clearly touched a nerve.

JAMIE: Can everyone just sit down and get on with something while the teachers sort this out.

HOLLY: Alright. No need to freak out.

They sit down.

Pause.

DOM absentmindedly taps out a rhythm on the desk. Slowly others join in. It gets more vigorous as they get into their drumming. BILLY calmly gets out a pair of noise cancelling headphones and puts them on.

JAMIE: Can you....just... not... you know.

DOM: (*Sarcastically*) Sorry, Miss!

Pause

DOM: Has anyone got any snacks?

HOLLY: What?

DOM: I'm hungry.

NADIA: We've just had lunch.

DOM: So? I'm starving.

ROSIE: I think I've got an apple.

DOM: No thanks.

HOLLY: Whose classroom is this?

NADIA: Miss Underwood's. Why?

HOLLY: She always has chocolate in her desk.

DOM: Seriously?

DOM starts going through the desk.

JAMIE: You can't just start rummaging through a teacher's desk.

DOM continues.

JAMIE: You absolutely cannot open that drawer.

DOM opens the drawer.

JAMIE: I forbid you from touching that chocolate.

DOM: Who wants a curly wurly?

ALEX: Have you got a wispa?

DOM throws a Curly Wurly to NADIA and a Wispa to ALEX.

HOLLY: I don't do carbs.

ALEX: What?

DOM: Rosie?

JAMIE: That's private property.

ROSIE: No. I'm vegan.

DOM: Billy?

BILLY lifts their head phones off one ear.

DOM: Curly Wurly?

BILLY: Nah. They're too sticky.

JAMIE: It's totally unacceptable! It's technically theft.

DOM: Alright. Calm down. It's only chocolate.

Pause

HOLLY: How do we know you're telling us the truth?

JAMIE: What?

HOLLY: You seem pretty worked up. How do we know that you're not the student who's had the 'incident?'

JAMIE: Don't be ridiculous.

ALEX: No. Think about it. That would make total sense.

JAMIE: How?

ALEX: You set the alarm off.

NADIA: You lock all of us in here and then pretend it's some other kid who's gone crazy.

ALEX: (*Dramatically*) You're holding us hostage.

ALEX takes a dramatic bite of his Wispa.

JAMIE: Oh, come on. Look at me. I'm obviously not...

ROSIE: (*Playfully*) I don't know. You hear about it all the time.

JAMIE: What?

ROSIE: These mega-brainy, high-flying students.

NADIA: Oh, yeah, the stress of exams.

ALEX: A Levels are meant to be super difficult.

HOLLY: And then the final blow.

JAMIE: What?

HOLLY: Being passed over for Head Prefect by Sweaty Hettie.

JAMIE: (*Losing control*) That was a year ago and don't call her that!

BILLY takes off their headphones and pays attention.

ALEX: Calm down. We're only joking.

JAMIE: Well, don't. OK?

ALEX: OK.

HOLLY: Sorry.

JAMIE: No. I'm sorry. I shouldn't have shouted. I just... I don't like being stuck in here any more than you do... And I'm not mega-brainy. Not really.

ROSIE: Well, you are... you're always getting called up in assembly to pick up some award or prize...

JAMIE scoffs.

NADIA: There's nothing wrong with that.

HOLLY: Yeah, I wish I was clever.

ROSIE: You are clever.

HOLLY: As if.

ROSIE: OK, so you're not going to win any maths prizes any time soon but you're one of the most creative people I know.

NADIA: Yeah, I wish I could draw or do make up like you

ROSIE: You're amazing.

HOLLY: You guys.

The girls hug. It's a wholesome friendship.

ALEX: (*To JAMIE*) What did you get in your GCSEs?

JAMIE: I did OK.

ALEX: No, come on. What did you get?

BILLY: They got four 8s and six 9s.

DOM: Wow!

JAMIE: How do you know that?

BILLY: It was in the Autumn newsletter.

ALEX: Who reads the school newsletter?

BILLY: I do.

JAMIE: Just because I got good grades doesn't mean I'm clever.

HOLLY: Err... I think it does.

JAMIE: No. I just work really, really hard.

HOLLY: Yeah, but I could revise for a hundred years and I still wouldn't be getting a 9 in maths!

JAMIE: Maybe you could. If you made it your priority. I've always been a perfectionist.

DOM: Like how?

JAMIE: Like, when I was in reception, all the other kids would come out with these pictures that they'd painted and I wouldn't have any. My mum asked my teacher about it and she said I was throwing them in the bin on the way out because I didn't think they were good enough.

ROSIE: Wow.

ALEX: That's pretty dark.

NADIA: Are your parents really pushy?

JAMIE: No. They're great. I was just wired that way. I like school.

DOM: Someone's got to.

JAMIE: It makes sense to me. I put the effort in and I get the grades. But then every time I get a good grade I put pressure on myself to get an even better grade next time.

DOM: What's that like?

JAMIE: Totally exhausting.

ROSIE: What do you do to relax? (*JAMIE thinks*)

JAMIE: Nothing.

ROSIE: Really?

JAMIE: Yeah, I do school. That's my 'thing'. There isn't anything else.

BILLY: That's really sad.

JAMIE: Yeah, I know. I'm a loser.

BILLY: Not sad as in 'pathetic' but sad as in 'unhappy'.

JAMIE snaps afraid they have exposed themselves too much.

JAMIE: The only thing that makes me unhappy is being stuck in here with you lot. Come on. Show time's over. Let's get back to whatever it is you were doing.

Everyone except BILLY retreats.

BILLY: Are you OK, Jamie?

JAMIE: I'm fine mate.

SCENE 2

Everything changes. We are in the world of what is unsaid inside JAMIE's head.

JAMIE: I'm not fine.

It's just something I say. Something we all say.

On autopilot.

Like saying it might make it true. One massive group delusion.

I'm not fine.

Stuck in this room.

I can feel it happening again. I'm becoming unstuck.

I need to hold it together. I'm not fine.

I'm not sure I have ever been fine. But I was, I think, doing OK.

Not great but OK.

I was OK.

Then when I was fourteen

With hormones dancing in my bloodstream

They locked down 'cause of Covid 19.

And I was left floating

Adrift.

Outside of myself and everything I knew

After a decade of school conditioning

My world turned askew.

Stuck in my room and learning online.

Disinfecting groceries.

Staying apart.

Endless updates as the numbers of dead

Just kept going up.

And no amount of maths revision

Could translate those numbers into dying figures.

And as the weeks and months drifted by

That painful first jolt of fear

Numbed into a dull, exhausting ache of anxiety.

So when we came back,

A brave new open world,

The feeling stuck with me.

And everything I thought I understood,

Learning, studying and revising,

Didn't make any sense anymore.

They call it a panic attack.

But not in the way you would expect.

So we sat down for our mock tests.

English lit. Our set texts.

And the fear floods through me.

Stomach flipping.

Heart beating.

Hands shaking.

But I'm not hyperventilating like you see on TV.

I can breathe just fine.

My body's not prepped up to fight

Or flight and runaway, Instead I freeze.

As everyone around me sits down and writes

I float somewhere else.

Adrift.

I cannot open my book.

I cannot pick up my pen.

I freeze.

I freeze 'cause I am not good enough.

I freeze with the fear that I cannot rip up my exam papers and throw them in the bin before anyone sees.

Miss Barton comes up and is being all nice.

Was I sick? Should I go see the nurse?

And I can't answer.

Frozen in ice.

And although since then I've had therapy,

To manage my stress,

Pass my exams,

And thaw out my insides,

I am still a mess.

Still trying to process what's happened to me and to the world I knew and understood.

And when something unexpected or unsettling happens,

I am straight back there.

Frozen in my mind.

The world snaps back to the now.

JAMIE: Honestly mate. I'm fine.

BILLY returns to their seat unconvinced.

SCENE 3

NADIA: What do you think's happened?

ROSIE: It's got to be something pretty big.

HOLLY: Maybe they set fire to the school!

ALEX: If they had then getting us to lock ourselves in classrooms wouldn't be the smartest move.

HOLLY: Oh, yeah.

ROSIE: I wouldn't put anything past Phipps.

DOM: You know what it could be?

ALEX: What?

DOM: Zombies.

BILLY: Zombies aren't real.

DOM: How do you know? They could be. Someone could have been infected and now they're roaming the corridors looking to eat human flesh.

He pretends to be a zombie and tries eating ALEX's arm.

ALEX: I'd say it's statistically unlikely.

DOM: Four years ago no one thought a pandemic would be a real thing and now look. Anything's possible.

HOLLY: Maybe they've got an OFSTED inspection and just want us out of the way.

ALEX: I could believe that for some of us (*indicting DOM*).

DOM: Hey!

ALEX: But Billy? Jamie? They're hardly going to bring the school into disrepute.

DOM: Right, so listen up. I heard that if the teacher doesn't turn up after 10 minutes we can legally, like legitimately, go home!

HOLLY: I thought it was fifteen minutes.

DOM: Either way time is almost up so I reckon we just leave 'em to it.

NADIA: Is that really true?

ALEX: I doubt it.

BILLY: That's a myth.

DOM: What?

BILLY: It's not a school rule. It's just a rumour.

DOM: Nah. Straight up. It is. My sister told me.

JAMIE: Even if it was true, which it's probably not, this isn't exactly a normal lesson situation. We just need to wait it out till it's all sorted.

ALEX: Wait what out?

They look to JAMIE expectantly.

Pause.

NADIA: He doesn't know.

ROSIE: What?

NADIA: He doesn't know what's going on either. He hasn't got a clue.

JAMIE: No... I do know. I mean I know a bit.

HOLLY: Prove it.

JAMIE: What?

HOLLY: If you're so keen to keep us here then you owe us an explanation. Come on.

Pause.

JAMIE: OK. But just keep it between us. Don't go posting anything on your phone.

HOLLY: I wouldn't.

JAMIE: Holly?

HOLLY: How do you know my name?

JAMIE: I'm not the only one whose reputation proceeds them.

HOLLY: OK. No phones.

She performatively turns off her phone and puts it in her bag.

JAMIE: OK, so I was walking down the East staircase when all these teachers started coming up the other way.

BILLY: But it's a one way system.

JAMIE: I know.

NADIA: Shhh

JAMIE: And they're actually running. And then suddenly Mr Phipps stops me and some other prefects and he's got a radio on him.

HOLLY: Standard.

JAMIE: And he tells us that, when the alarm goes off, we should split off into different classrooms and make sure any younger kids stay put until a teacher comes.

And I can hear all these voices over his radio and they're saying that some kid in year 10 has had some kind of episode.

DOM: What?

ALEX: What do you mean 'episode'?

JAMIE: That's all they said.

DOM: Someone's obviously lost it.

NADIA: Lost it?

HOLLY: They mean someone's had some kind of mental health problem.

NADIA: Why would that put us in lockdown?

DOM: Maybe they're dangerous?

NADIA: Really?

ROSIE: It's much more likely that they're trying to hurt themselves than someone else.

DOM: Either way. It's pretty inconsiderate.

HOLLY: What?

DOM: I've got Rugby practice in twenty minutes.

HOLLY: (*To DOM*) You're unbelievable.

DOM: Thank you.

ALEX: As long as you've got your priorities right.

DOM: (*To JAMIE*) Come on they must have said who it was.

JAMIE: I'm not saying any more. OK. It's none of our business.

ALEX: OK.

ROSIE: Yeah, fair enough.

SCENE 4

DOM: Would you rather have hands for feet or feet for hands?

ALEX: Erghh... I hate feet. Definitely hands for feet.

ROSIE: Obviously hands for feet.

NADIA: No contest.

DOM: (*Winding up ALEX*) Yeah, but think how much you could freak people out if you had big old feet hands. You'd be a TikTok sensation. Channel 5 love that stuff.

ALEX: Stop it. Blurgh.

ALEX: OK. OK. I've got one. Would you rather speak every human language or be able to speak to all animals?

BILLY: Obviously I'd speak to animals.

NADIA: Human definitely.

ROSIE: Really?

HOLLY: Yeah, imagine if you went on holiday and could just chat up anyone you wanted around the pool.

ROSIE: OK but imagine what you could discover if you could understand animals.

ALEX: Yeah, but what if you didn't like what they had to say? (*To DOM*) What if your dog secretly hated you?

DOM: No way. Have you seen the way his little face looks at me? That dude loves me. I don't need no doggy language to prove it.

BILLY: What breed of dog have you got?

DOM: He's a cockapoo.

BILLY: Oh, I love cockapoos. I've got a covapoo. He's called Rudie. I've had him since he was a puppy and he's eight now. I got him when I was six and he's just the best dog ever. I've got a photo here.

BILLY shows DOM a keyring with their dog on it.

BILLY: I would absolutely love to be able to talk to him. I talk to him all the time but I'd love for him to talk back.

DOM awkwardly hands back the keyring.

BILLY: When I'm stressed it's like he knows and he sits on my lap and just lets me stroke him.

The social interaction is off and DOM feels awkward. BILLY returns to their seat.

DOM: Cool.

Pause.

NADIA: OK, I've got one. Would you rather be clever but ugly or stupid and beautiful?

ALEX: Clever and ugly. Hmm. No wait.

ROSIE: Obviously clever. Think what you could do if you were really smart. You could cure cancer, end global warming.

ALEX: How ugly are we talking about?

HOLLY: I'd rather be pretty but braindead. May as well stick with what I know.

ROSIE: Stop it.

NADIA: Jamie?

JAMIE: What?

NADIA: Would you rather be clever but ugly or stupid and beautiful?

JAMIE: Easy. Looks fade. I'd rather be clever.

ROSIE: So does intelligence. Your brain cells literally start dying off when you get old.

DOM: Alright. Alright. Would you rather have a finger as a tongue or tongues for fingers?

HOLLY: Eurggh, that's even worse!

HOLLY and NADIA mess about pretending to kiss with finger tongues. ROSIE is left out. ROSIE wants HOLLY's attention so grabs a ball of paper.

ROSIE: Hey Holly. Think fast!

HOLLY and ROSIE enjoy throwing the paper ball. JAMIE is annoyed. After a few catches ROSIE drops it.

HOLLY: In the middle.

ROSIE reluctantly goes in the middle. HOLLY and NADIA throw it over her head quite a few times and she is unable to catch it.

SCENE 5

Suddenly we are in the world of what is unsaid inside ROSIE's head.

ROSIE: I like Nadia. I really do. She's funny and forthright and just comes out with stuff and says it which is great.

But ever since she's been around it's not been the same. She and Holly just click and I'm the one whose left out.

And sometimes they look at me and I think they hate me.

It used to be so easy with Holly.

The summer before secondary she spent so much time at mine that she actually kept a toothbrush there.

We would just look into each others eyes and know what the other was thinking. But now I've changed... we both have.

I can't talk to her like before.

I don't tell her all the things I'm thinking because I don't know how she'd react. What if I'm too much and push her away.

So, I perform this sort of half person.

A version of myself I think she will like and...

ROSIE finally catches the ball. The world snaps back to the now and HOLLY returns to the previous 'would you rather,' game.

SCENE 6

HOLLY: OK. Would you rather have the ability to rewind your life or pause it?

NADIA: Pause it.

ROSIE: Depends. How far back can you rewind?

HOLLY: How far back do you want to rewind?

ROSIE: Maybe the sixties or earlier. Turn of the twentieth century?

HOLLY: This isn't time travel. It's got to be in your life time.

ROSIE: Right, yeah, sorry.

ALEX: I'd rewind.

HOLLY: To when?

ALEX: Maybe to when I was six or seven.

HOLLY: One hundred percent! You could spend a whole afternoon just scrunching up little bits of tissue paper and sticking. I miss that.

NADIA: You could still do that.

HOLLY: And ruin my nails. No chance.

ROSIE: Do you remember we spent absolutely ages making that card to send to Kate and Will to congratulate them on the birth of princess Charlotte?

HOLLY: We took it so seriously. Oooh and you ended up with PVA glue all over your arm and we convinced Miss Ahmed that your skin was peeling off and she made you go to the nurse.

ROSIE and HOLLY giggle. NADIA is left out.

To regain HOLLY's attention NADIA grabs the ball and restarts the game.

NADIA: Hey Holly. Think fast.

Again the girls play. When NADIA drops it she is placed in the middle.

HOLLY: In the middle.

SCENE 7

We shift to the world of what is unsaid inside NADIA's head.

NADIA: Even here, playing this game, surrounded by people, I still feel alone.

Like I don't belong.

Or they are just letting me join in because they feel sorry for me. I know I can never be the kind of friend to Holly that Rosie is.

They've known each other a long time.

They speak the same language.

In the UK most people don't say hello or hi. They just say 'you alright?'

And at first I didn't get it. I thought I must look like there was something wrong with me but then I realised they are not actually asking if I am alright. They don't want to know.

And I miss my friends back home and I'm devastated that we never got to say goodbye.

And I haven't told anyone what happened to bring me here. I can't.

I can't tell them what it was like to live in constant fear.

Never knowing who I could trust. Always alert.

Vigilant.

Waiting for that knock on the door.

I can't tell them that we left in the middle of the night. Cooped up like animals.

Like criminals.

Just because my Mum wrote an article for a newspaper and it told the truth. They haven't asked...

And I haven't told my story because it might be too much for them to bear.

And I don't want to take that risk.

So I shut off that part of myself and think to the future and...

JAMIE catches the ball. The world snaps back to the now

JAMIE: Enough - Some of us are trying to work!

DOM: Buzz kill.

Reluctantly everyone sits down.

SCENE 8

DOM: OK, err would you rather... eat the same meal every night or give up social media?

ALEX: That's a tough one.

BILLY: I'd eat the same meal.

HOLLY: But you barely use social media.

BILLY: Yeah, but I more or less eat the same thing every night anyway.

HOLLY: True.

BILLY: It would save on arguments.

ALEX: I'd be so bored without my socials.

JAMIE: No prizes for what Holly's going to choose.

HOLLY: What's that supposed to mean?

JAMIE: Nothing.

ALEX: He means you're insta-famous, darling.

JAMIE: Exactly. Maybe if you spend a bit less time online and a bit more doing your school work then...

HOLLY: What?

NADIA: You've got to admit you do post a lot.

JAMIE: If you don't want people judging you then maybe curb it a bit.

HOLLY is upset. JAMIE realises they've gone too far.

JAMIE: I didn't mean anything by it.

HOLLY: You did.

ROSIE: If you ask me it's a bit creepy. Some sixth former stalking a year 9 online.

JAMIE: I'm not... stalking... it's just... it's cropped up on my feed.

HOLLY: Do you all think I'm shallow?

JAMIE: I didn't say that.

ROSIE: No.

DOM: Kind of.

HOLLY: Right. I see.

NADIA: Holly.

HOLLY: No. That's great. Absolutely fantastic.

ALEX: Babe.

HOLLY: Least I know where I stand.

SCENE 9

Everything changes. We are in the world of what is unsaid inside HOLLY's head. Images and ideas move fast here and fly into each other.

HOLLY: Elizabeth the first inspired a generation of women to poison themselves with toxic lead on their skin?

During the renaissance, Italian women blinded themselves with deadly nightshade to make their pupils look bigger.

In the 1800s women would synch their waists with corsets so tight that their deformed rib cages actually stopped them breathing.

The ancient practice of foot binding in China left women struggling to walk.

In the Victorian era women made themselves sick by digesting tape worms which literally ate them up from the inside.

Gross.

Using Instagram has been proven in countless studies, over and over again, to be linked to an increase in teenage girls with eating disorders...

To anxiety.

To depression.

And to suicide.

I know that.

We were taught about it at school.

My mum made me watch some documentary on TV.

That's not the whole story...

'Cause even though it's damaging and just as toxic as any trends that came before

I. Absolutely. Love It!

I can spend hours completely absorbed. Choosing my angles.

My set up.

My lighting. Blurring, Concealing, Contouring, Highlighting, Shaping.

Colouring myself in.

Cropping.

Filtering. Reimagining.

Wording, rephrasing, curating. I am my own canvas.

Endless reincarnations. I am my own work of art.

And I know that every new follower, every new like,

Sets me alight.

And the pace,

The way it moves and evolves,

An ever-changing stream of aesthetic data, To consume, comment and curate.

I don't know if it just works with the way I think or if it has shaped the way I think,

But it gives me a buzz.

So I keep scrolling and scrolling.

When I wake up every morning the first thing I do is check my phone And when I fall asleep my phone is still in my hand

Because it makes me feel... exhausted.

Overwhelmed.

But connected.

Like I am part of something... important.

Like I am worth more than my rubbish school report.

And I can ignore all those idiots who make nasty comments 'cause haters gotta hate but lovers...

I honestly feel like some of my best friends are those I made online. And I know that's a risk,

Because we can all be anyone we like online, But that's also the beauty.

I can hide behind my wall.

And yes it can be exploited.

To groom...

To bully...

And to spread hate.

But it can also be harnessed to tell a different narrative. To find your people and reclaim your story.

OK, so when a plus-size influencer posts a picture that slays without apologising for her body she may not break the beauty mould but she chips away at it.

When enough of us posted hashtag metoo or hashtag everyone's invited we may not have knocked patriarchy completely off its course but we have steered a new direction.

And posting a little black square and not doing anything else may be nothing more than virtue signally but now a whole generation know the words Black Lives Matter and that's worth something.

SCENE 10

The world snaps back to the now.

NADIA: Is it a boy or a girl?

JAMIE: I can't say?

ALEX: Because you don't want to tell us or because you can't assume their gender?

JAMIE: Both.

ALEX: So it's someone in year 10 who is gender non-conforming.

JAMIE: I didn't say that.

DOM: Probably is though.

ALEX: Why?

DOM: You know I'm not homophobic.

HOLLY: Well obviously.

DOM: What?

HOLLY: We just assumed you and Alex were boyfriends.

DOM: No! I mean not that that would be a problem. I'm an ally. But we're not... Alex tell them...

ALEX: (*Tongue in cheek*) Are you breaking up with me?

The group laugh.

DOM: I hate all of you.

ALEX: Oh sugarcakes, you're breaking me heart.

DOM: What I was trying to say was that you have to admit... your lot, well, you are all a little bit... sensitive.

ALEX looks incredulously at DOM.

DOM: Well, you are!!!

ALEX: I didn't realise when I was getting ready for school today that I would need to represent the entire LGBTQ population.

DOM: I'm just saying it's more likely to be one of your friends than one of the rugby lads.

ALEX: Really.

NADIA: 'Cause gay lads can't play rugby?

BILLY: All that cuddling up.

DOM: It's called a scrum.

BILLY: You'd think being gay would be an advantage.

BILLY goes back to their book. HOLLY, NADIA and ROSIE laugh.

DOM: I didn't mean anything bad by it just...

ALEX: Sure.

DOM: Alex! Don't get all moody.

HOLLY: A lover's tiff?

ALEX: Just let it go.

SCENE 11

Everything changes. We are in the world of what is unsaid inside ALEX's head.

ALEX: But it's me that's letting it go... again.

And it's... Just. So. Tiring. When Dom says things like that, When we're shoved all together Like we're all the same.

When Dom claims to be an ally...

But then acts all disgusted at the idea that I could be his boyfriend. Tells me to be proud...

But then does something that proves he thinks it's shameful. It's so absolutely. Completely. Exhausting.

And even thinking that I feel guilty. I have no right to complain...

When those who came before had to fight for my right to exist. When even now, across the world, I am illegal in seventy countries.

I. Should. Be. Grateful.

Because. We have it good.

We don't have to hide who we are or who we love just to get a job.

Our teachers don't have to censor themselves for fear of promoting the acceptability of homosexuality.

I can get married.

I can adopt a child.

But I am still the only grandchild who couldn't bring their boyfriend to Grandma's 80th.

In case it upset her or some cousin or uncle. To protect me.

Just in case.

I can walk down the street and not fear for my life... Usually.

Except for the time I was followed back from the train station to my sister's flat. Three lads chased me up the stairs and I only just made it inside in time.

Their fingers curling around the edge of the door as I slammed it. Shaking as they shouted through the letterbox while we called the police. But that was the exception.

There has never been a better time in modern history to be gay or a 'they'

But yeah. It could well be one of 'my lot' whose mental health has floundered. But cut us some slack.

Because for all the progression we are still held back...

Not by overt persecution or tyrannical laws...

But by hundreds of tiny assumptions and aggressions... Tiny cuts.

We may not be walking wounded but we are still battle-scarred. And I carry the fear of rejection each time we have to out ourselves. I carry the weight of having to speak up for my friends...

The pressure of correcting pronouns and unhelpful assumptions,

The responsibility of speaking up and out for a community so vast and diverse that I will never get it right for everyone.

But still I try.

To honour those brave warriors who fought before... And to keep fighting for those who follow.

The world snaps back to the now.

DOM: Mate....I really didn't mean to....

ALEX: I know.

DOM: We good?

ALEX: Yeah, all good.

SCENE 12

ROSIE: Who do you reckon it is?

NADIA: I don't really know anyone in year 10 that well, so...

HOLLY: Maybe Summer?

ROSIE: Oh, yeah, I didn't think of her but... maybe.

NADIA: Who's Summer?

ROSIE: You know... she's really pretty. She's got long hair and usually wears in it a plait.

Massively into Pokemon?

NADIA: Maybe? Why her?

HOLLY: She had to have loads of time off last year because she had an eating disorder.

NADIA: I don't think that's relevant.

ROSIE: I thought she was better now though.

HOLLY: What's her surname?

ROSIE: Err... Hunter, I think.

HOLLY types it into her phone.

HOLLY: Not her!

NADIA: How'd you know?

HOLLY: She's just posted. Look. A load of year 10s are in the science block.

ROSIE: What about George?

NADIA: Which one's George?

ROSIE: You know George. They're the one who's always got a Covid mask on.

NADIA: Really? Even now?

ROSIE: Exactly!

HOLLY: They're not the type.

NADIA: What about Jess?

ROSIE: Who?

NADIA: New girl.

BILLY buts in.

BILLY: It won't be Jess.

NADIA: She does seem a bit weird.

HOLLY: Do you know her?

BILLY: Yeah, we're helping Miss Sparkes with the set for the school play.

HOLLY: And she's always got that woman following her around.

BILLY: Her learning support assistant!

NADIA: They must be pretty worried about her if she needs that much supervision!

BILLY: Or maybe she just needs that much support with her learning! It's not her. She's really shy. The last thing she'd want to do is cause a scene.

ROSIE: Ooh, I know... what about Dylan?

HOLLY: Dylan McKenzie. Yeah could be.

NADIA: Who's Dylan?

HOLLY: You won't know 'cause it was before you joined, but when we were in year 7 he kept setting the fire alarm off and throwing chairs. He was completely out of control.

BILLY: Hadn't his brother just died?

NADIA: That's quite a long time ago.

ROSIE: Yeah but you've got to admit he's got form.

HOLLY starts looking up DYLAN on her phone but sees something else.

HOLLY: Oh my God!

ROSIE: What?

HOLLY: Look!

HOLLY shows the two girls her phone and suddenly the three are running to the window.

BILLY: What are you doing?

JAMIE: Come away from the window.

The girls ignore him and the rest of the group also rush.

JAMIE: I mean it. Sit down!

HOLLY: Can you see anything?

BILLY: Nothing.

DOM: Let me.

JAMIE: Guys...

BILLY: There's nothing to see...

DOM: Let me.....

JAMIE: (*Giving up slightly*) Well?

DOM: ...Nothing.

BILLY: Told you.

DOM: What are we looking for?

NADIA: Apparently there's a girl on the roof.

ALEX: Where?

DOM: I can't see anything.

ALEX: There's nothing there.

Slowly the group move away from the window.

DOM: Maybe she jumped already.

ROSIE: Dom! That's horrible.

DOM: I was just saying.

ALEX: Well, maybe don't just say.

BILLY: (*Genuinely concerned*) You'd have to be really desperate to go up on the roof.

JAMIE: There's no one on the roof.

BILLY: But she said...

JAMIE: (*Quietly*) Look Holly probably just made it up for attention.

BILLY: (*A little too loud*) Holly wouldn't do that.

HOLLY: Do what?

BILLY: Jamie's saying you made up the thing about the roof for attention. Then I said you wouldn't do that because you wouldn't lie about something like that.

HOLLY: Thanks, Billy.

DOM: Urgggh, How long do you think they'll make us stay here?

JAMIE: Look, they're probably just waiting for an ambulance to come...

BILLY: An ambulance?

JAMIE: Or the police.

BILLY: I don't like hospitals.

DOM: What are the police gonna do about it?

JAMIE: I dunno the fire brigade?

HOLLY: Firemen. Where?

HOLLY and ALEX jump up enthusiastically.

BILLY: Will they have to go to hospital?

DOM: (*Sarcastically*) Oooh, firemen. Where?

NADIA: Or fireladies.

JAMIE: I think the term might be fire fighters.

DOM: But there's no fire.

ALEX: OK.

DOM: So, no fire fighters to be seen.

HOLLY: Shame.

ROSIE: It's really quiet.

NADIA: Yeah, there's no one out there. It's a bit creepy.

They look out of the window.

BILLY: I quite like it like this.

ROSIE: Really?

BILLY: It's calmer. Stops my brain feeling so noisy.

ROSIE: But it's too still. Even the leaves on the trees aren't moving. It's like the trees and the playground and the wind and even the birds are waiting.

BILLY: Waiting for what?

ROSIE: It's so still it doesn't look real.

HOLLY: Stop it. You've given me goosebumps. Look at my arm.

ROSIE: Like it's all waiting for something to happen.

BILLY: Like what?

ROSIE: I don't know but we can't stop it.

There is a feeling of foreboding in the air. The group move away from the window leaving ROSIE alone.

SCENE 13

Everything changes. We are in the world of what is unsaid inside ROSIE's head.

ROSIE: Out the window everything I look at is a constant reminder of the undeniable, absolutely irrefutable truth...

Species are dying, oceans are rising and this planet will become completely uninhabitable.

And that existential dread keeps burning in my brain.

Everything I look at is a reminder that we are doomed.

The one-use plastics and coffee cups littering the pavement outside.

The cars idling in the traffic jam just beyond the school gates spitting out their putrid gas so we can't breathe.

Without thinking I reach out and the cold glass touches my

fingers and my hand leaves a mark on the window.

And I look at the dirty hand print between me and the still trees.

And I want to apologise. I want to say look, Mr Tree, I'm sorry that we've broken the planet but it wasn't me. My generation are just paying the price for my parents or their parents. It was so incredibly obvious that we couldn't keep consuming and burning at such a rate and that there would be consequences.

And I feel completely useless and I hate that I feel like I can't do anything.

I think I am losing my mind because I'm not some kind of hippy freak but then I might as well talk to the trees and the air and the birds and the sky because no one else is listening.

And I get it. I know why no one wants to listen because we are all just numb to it.

But when Holly buys her latest look from Shein or Nadia sits there eating some greasy burger it's like there is a silent scream constantly echoing in my skull and no one is coming to save us.

No amount of recycling or veganism is going to stop the inevitable complete and utter destruction of the world.

SCENE 14

The world snaps back to the now.

BILLY: Excuse me, Jamie Sinclair. How long do you think we'll be here for?

JAMIE: Probably not too much longer.

BILLY: I've got art club at three thirty so...

ROSIE: Actually I need to pick up my little brother.

BILLY: Miss Sparkes will be wondering where I am.

DOM: What about me? I've got Rugby.

BILLY: We're painting the sets for the 'A Midsummer Night's Dream'.

DOM: We've got a big match coming up.

JAMIE: You're all just going to have to be patient.. Please sit down.

BILLY sits down but is clearly uncomfortable. The others do the same.

HOLLY: Hey Billy. You OK?

She does a thumbs up. BILLY responds with a so-so hand gesture. HOLLY gently approaches BILLY but gives them space.

HOLLY: Why... (*she does the so-so hand gesture*) Too many plan changes?

BILLY nods.

HOLLY: OK. What can I do?

BILLY writes in their notebook.

HOLLY: I can't get you to art. I wish I could.

DOM: What's wrong with them?

HOLLY: Just butt out ok?

HOLLY rummages through her bag and finds a clear pencil case of fidgets.

HOLLY: Fidget?

BILLY chooses a fidget.

JAMIE: I said to sit...

Mid-sentence JAMIE realises that BILLY is not OK.

JAMIE: What's wrong. Are they sick?

DOM: Are they diabetic? We've got chocolate.

HOLLY: No they're fine. Billy? Do you want your headphones?

BILLY nods.

DOM: Why aren't they talking?

HOLLY: Your hoody?

BILLY nods.

HOLLY: They just need a break? Billy? Do you want me to stay or go?

As she says stay and go she signs each word. BILLY signs back go.

HOLLY: They need some space.

She calmly leaves and JAMIE goes after her.

JAMIE: How did you know what to do?

HOLLY: Maybe there's more to me than you thought.

JAMIE: OK. Yeah. I'm sorry. You were brilliant with them.

HOLLY: Yeah, well, Billy's my mate and we've been friends since year 5 so we've worked out a system.

JAMIE: You're a really good friend.

HOLLY: It's a pretty small thing to do for someone you care about.

JAMIE: So in the future if someone who's...

HOLLY: Neurodivergent...

JAMIE: Like Billy...is having a ...

HOLLY: Shut down?

JAMIE: That's what I should do?

HOLLY: Not necessarily.

JAMIE: No?

HOLLY: Billy's just one Autistic person. They're an individual.

JAMIE: OK.

HOLLY: So for Billy, plans and routines are really important. And they've got so much better at managing it but today... this afternoon... too many changes all at once so they need to kind of recalibrate their system.

JAMIE: So...

HOLLY: So for Billy, that usually means reducing noise, offering something to keep their hands busy and items that they find comforting.

JAMIE: OK, How do you know this?

HOLLY: Billy and me talked about it when they weren't feeling overwhelmed so they were able to tell me.

JAMIE: When it happens what do you think's happening inside their head?

SCENE 15

Everything changes. We are in the world of what is unsaid inside BILLY's head.

BILLY: I know they're talking about me.

I don't care.

It doesn't matter. I can see.

I can hear.

But I am not here.

Obviously am physically here. But mentally

I have cast a spell.

I have conjured an iridescent bubble... to hold me.

Glinda the Good Witch has got nothing on me.

I am enclosed.

I am safe.

And because I have closed off from the outside,

Just for a bit,

I can start to untangle the afternoon. That alarm was loud.

Really loud.

And it's not like I'm some mad bat with ultrasonic hearing, But my whole body resonated.

I am the resonator!

I can still feel it under my skin. And the sound means danger.

So even though they said it's nothing to worry about,

There is danger still under my skin.

And Dom made those stupid assumptions.

And that hurt Alex a bit

And I feel his feelings

And Jamie said that stuff to Holly

And I know that it got to her because I can feel it.

And I don't know exactly what's wrong with Nadia

But I can sense her hurting

And someone might or might not be up on the roof but I can still feel their pain.

My ultrasonic power picks up everything. The hum from the fluorescent lights.

The invasion of prying eyes.

People think if you're Autistic you don't feel anything

But for me I feel it all too much.

And there is nothing I can do and nowhere I can go so instead I shut down.

I cast my spell.

I conjure my bubble.

And I wait it out.

SCENE 16

The world snaps back to the now. BILLLY is recovered from their shut down.

BILLY: I'm feeling better now.

JAMIE: You gave us a bit of a fright there.

BILLY: Sorry. I just had a plan in my head and then when everything kept changing...

HOLLY: You don't have to apologise.

BILLY: I know. It's just embarrassing with people who don't know me so well. Being on time is really important to me.

JAMIE: Don't worry we get it.

DOM: I think we're all a little bit Autistic really?

BILLY and their friends groan.

BILLY: (*Exasperated*) What?!

HOLLY: That's like saying someone is a little bit pregnant.

DOM: Yeah, but what I mean is...

BILLY: You basically are or you aren't.

DOM: But what about people who don't find out till they're an adult?

BILLY: They were always Autistic. They just hadn't been diagnosed yet.

ROSIE: And, while you're at it, just 'cause someone likes things being neat, it doesn't mean they've got OCD.

NADIA: Or if they're having mood swings that they've got a personality disorder.

ALEX: Or if they're being selfish, they're a narcissist.

HOLLY is riffling through her disorganised bag. Dropping things.

HOLLY: If they're really disorganised it doesn't mean that they have ADHD.

ROSIE picks up HOLLY's processions for her.

ROSIE: I mean you do have ADHD.

HOLLY: I know I do. I'm just saying not all disorganised people do.

JAMIE: And you can't really go around diagnosing yourself or other people just because of some TikTok video you've watched.

HOLLY: Exactly!

ROSIE: But isn't that how you realised you were...?

HOLLY: Yes OK, fine, but I got it confirmed. Had a proper diagnosis.

DOM: Alright, OK... no need to go off on one. You can't say anything these days. I'm well depressed.

The group react to DOM's use of the word 'depressed', walking off and leaving him with JAMIE.

DOM: What?

JAMIE: You're not depressed! You might be annoyed or sad but those are just feelings. Everyone has them and then they pass and you start feeling something else. Depression is much more than that.

DOM: Right OK.. There's no need to have a go at me.

JAMIE: I'm not.

DOM: It's just... I don't know...

JAMIE: Tell me.

DOM: How do you know?

JAMIE: What?

DOM: When something's just a feeling or something more? I'm always feeling stuff.

JAMIE: Of course you are.

DOM: What's that supposed to mean?

JAMIE: How old are you? Fourteen?

DOM: Yeah. I suppose you're going to blame hormones.

JAMIE: Well, obviously, but it's more than that. The bit of your brain that's responsible for emotions that's called the amygdala right? And during the teenage years it goes into overdrive and it's not properly linked to the logical bit yet so that's why teenagers... we can be a bit dramatic.

DOM: How do you know this stuff?

JAMIE: I'm taking psychology... it's part of my extended... EPQ. But it's not even just the brain chemistry stuff. It's all the other things.

DOM: Like what?

JAMIE: Think about it. We've got a school system with more high-stakes tests than anywhere in Europe. We're connected twenty four seven to everyone and everything. We can't switch off. There's been the first global pandemic in over a hundred years. There's wars and censorship and fake news. Everyone's worried about whether to put their heating on and the cost of food and on top of that... we're literally living on a dying planet in the grip of climate change!

Suddenly JAMIE realises that everyone is listening.

JAMIE: So, it's not really surprising that our generation would be struggling. It's a sane response to an insane world.

DOM: But if everyone is feeling all this stuff all the time how are we supposed to know when it's something to worry about?

JAMIE: I suppose it's when the negative feelings don't change or get worse over time. If they stop you doing what you want to do. Or if someone's personality or behaviour changes. If they're usually someone who likes going out all the time and suddenly they're in their room and won't talk to anyone.

BILLY: I told you he was brainy.

SCENE 17

DOM: Jamie?

JAMIE: What?

DOM: I need a wee.

JAMIE: Well, you're just gonna have to hold it.

DOM: Look. There's a toilet just at the end of the corridor. I can be there and back in a minute.

ALEX: Maybe two if he washes his hands.

JAMIE: I'm sure this will be resolved really soon but until then...

DOM: But that's like an infringement of my human rights.

JAMIE: Look, I'm just doing what I've been told...

DOM: That's what they said in Nazi Germany.

ALEX: Of course it would be far worse if we reminded you of running water. Waterfalls.

Psssssssss.

DOM: What if I've got some kind of medical condition that means I can't hold it?

ALEX: He doesn't.

DOM: How do you know?

JAMIE: Do you have some kind of medical condition?

DOM: I might.

JAMIE: And what might this medical condition be called?

DOM: Piddlius urinitus.

JAMIE: Just do something to take your mind off it.

ALEX: Psss... psss... pssssssss...

DOM: (*Playfully*) What would you do if I chose to ignore your advice?

JAMIE: Well, I'd...

DOM: I could do. I could stand up. I am standing up.

He stands up.

JAMIE: Stop it.

DOM: I could walk towards the door. Oh, look. I'm walking.

DOM starts to walk.

JAMIE: And I could block way.

JAMIE stands up.

DOM: And I could reach out for the door handle.

DOM starts rattling the door handle.

JAMIE: Then I'd have to physically stop you.

JAMIE places their hands firmly but playfully on DOM's shoulders.

DOM: And I'd struggle because my bladder might be weak but my will is strong.

Help! Help!

JAMIE: Cut it out.

DOM: Help! My piddlius overflowius!

The group laughs but NADIA isn't finding it funny.

NADIA: Get off him!

ROSIE: They're only messing about.

NADIA: I said get off him.

JAMIE: OK, calm down.

HOLLY: It was just a joke. Nads?

SCENE 18

Everything changes. We are in the world of what is unsaid inside NADIA's head.

NADIA: And the floor falls away from under me

And straight away I am back there.

And it's like the last fourteen months in the UK haven't happened And I am back there.

In my country.

Before we left.

The smell of books burning still lingering in the air. My lips pressed hard together to stifle a scream.

The guards are outside and they're rattling the door handle as we sneak out the back into the cold night air. And my Mum and Dad and me...

We run.

And the sound of my aunt trying to stall them is carried on the wind as we reach the road where my Dad's colleague's vehicle is waiting.

And we are in the back of the van and hiding under blankets. And I can smell petrol and sweat and my Mum's perfume.

And I don't breathe as the van lurches to a stop and I can hear voices outside.

And I don't breathe...

As the sound of the back opening almost deafens me. And I don't breathe...

As, even under the blankets, the sweeping torch light almost blinds me. And I don't breathe...

Until the doors are closed and the van accelerates into the night. And I look over and I see that my father is silently sobbing.

And I have never seen him cry before.

And I want to comfort him but I have no words. And we cross the boarder to safety.

But still we are constantly looking over our shoulders

And we have lost everything we had and I am leaving everything and everyone I know.

SCENE 19

The world snaps back to the now but NADIA is still reliving her experience. She is disconnected and breathing heavily.

JAMIE: Holly. Do something.

HOLLY: I don't know what to do.

ROSIE: Nadia? Are you OK?

DOM: Someone get her a fidget.

BILLY: That won't help.

NADIA is distressed, immersed in her flashback

ROSIE: Nad's, it's OK. Nadia. Can you hear me? I don't know what's happening for you at the moment but I'm here and Holly's here and we're here for you and you're safe, OK?

ROSIE: I'm just going to sit here.

I'm going to take some deep breaths. Nice and slowly.

Can you look at me?

NADIA looks at ROSIE.

ROSIE: In and out. In and out. Good.

In and out?

We're in a geography classroom. At school.

Can you see that?

NADIA: Yeah.

ROSIE: Good. What can you see?

NADIA: I can see Billy's headset.

ROSIE: What else?

NADIA: The chocolate wrapper.

ROSIE: Yes.

NADIA: And the cactus on Miss Underwood's desk.

ROSIE: Yeah that's right. What about your hands. What can you feel?

NADIA: The floor. It's really dirty.

ROSIE: Yeah. Can you hear anything?

NADIA: The traffic outside.

ROSIE: Yes.

NADIA: And your voice.

I'm sorry. I didn't mean to...

ROSIE: It's OK.

NADIA: I can't...explain.

ROSIE: It's OK. You don't have to.

SCENE 20

Everyone tries to act normal.

ALEX: You OK?

ROSIE: Yeah.

ALEX: Sure?

ROSIE: A bit shaken up but better now Nadia's OK.

ALEX: You did really well.

ALEX hugs ROSIE.

ROSIE: Thanks.

ALEX: Do you know why she...?

ROSIE: No. She'll tell us if she wants to.

Pause.

ALEX: You know I really admire you.

ROSIE: What?

ALEX: Seriously.

ROSIE: For what?

ALEX: Living by your principles.

ROSIE: ...?

ALEX: Foregoing chocolate in the name of veganism. I'd never have the willpower.

DOM: You can get vegan chocolate.

ROSIE: Yeah, but then you have to make certain it's been ethically sourced, no workers have been exploited. Do you know some of it has palm oil in it and, although that's not technically an animal product, it still has a really detrimental effect on our environment.

ALEX: That's what I mean.

DOM: And bacon. That's what I said to my sister. I said Nancy, how can you give up bacon?

ROSIE: Well, you can do this thing with rice paper in an air-fryer...

ALEX: And cheese! I love cheese. Sorry Ro, but no amount of nutritional yeast is gonna cut it. And have you smelt vegan cheese? Uggh.

ROSIE: It's not that bad.

DOM: I'm getting hungry now.

ALEX: You've just eaten.

He goes over to the drawer again.

JAMIE: Really?

DOM: I'll sort it with Miss Underwood later. She won't mind. I'm one of her favourites... What? I am.

ALEX: If you say so.

DOM: (*To JAMIE in a tempting fashion*) KitKat Chunky? You know you want to.

JAMIE: OK. But on the strict understanding that we're replacing it after.

DOM: Scout's honour... What? I could be a scout.

DOM gets out the last chocolate bar. He looks like he is about to open it but then thinks better of it.

DOM: Err. Nadia? Erm would you like this? It's the last one.

NADIA: Don't you want it?

DOM: It's cool. Cool beans. You can have it.

He hands her the chocolate bar and leaves awkwardly.

NADIA: Thanks.

SCENE 21

DOM: Jamie?

JAMIE: Yes

DOM: Let's say I've got this friend...

JAMIE: Right. OK.

DOM: And this friend of mine, well, they're a friend of a friend really. I don't know them that well..

JAMIE: Sure...

DOM: If anything they're an acquaintance.

JAMIE: OK, so what's going on with this acquaintance?

DOM: They're just... Their moods seem really off. Like one minute they're really happy and pleased to see me and the next they're accusing me of all sorts of stuff.
And their parents don't really know what to do.

ALEX: You know their parents?

DOM: And she keeps saying that she's not safe and she won't come out of her room and she won't eat with anyone...

ALEX: Who is this?

DOM: You don't know them.

JAMIE: I'm not an expert but it sounds like she probably does need to see a professional to get some help.

DOM: Right. Yeah.

JAMIE: Maybe you could suggest that?

DOM: Yeah.

He goes to walk away.

JAMIE: Seriously, if your mate is struggling you really do need to get them some help.

DOM: Like I say I don't really know them so...

JAMIE: Take this year 11 girl, if someone had flagged up what was going on with her then things might not have gone this far.

DOM: You said year 10.

JAMIE: Did I?

DOM: They did, didn't they?

NADIA: I think so.

HOLLY: Definitely

JAMIE: I dunno. Probably? Maybe? Yes?

DOM: (*To JAMIE*) You did. You said a load of teachers went running up the stairs and then you heard on Phipps' radio that it was some kid in year 10.

JAMIE: I can't remember.

DOM: Well, what was it? Year 10 or year 11?

HOLLY: Wooah, calm down. What's the big deal?

ALEX: (*Suddenly realising*) Nancy.

ROSIE: What?

ALEX: His sister's in year 11.

SCENE 22

The crisis of the situation causes DOM to unmask. He panics and desperately wants to leave the room.

DOM: Nancy. Nancy!

He runs to the door and tries to leave but is stopped by JAMIE and ALEX.

DOM: Get out my way!

ALEX: We can't.

JAMIE: Just stay calm.

DOM: My sister is on the roof and you're telling me to stay calm!

ALEX: You don't know that.

DOM: I do. It's her. It's got to be. (*Distraught*) You don't understand. You have to let me go!

The rest of the group look out of the window.

BILLY: There's someone up there.

NADIA: Dom? You need to see this.

DOM turns to look and realises immediately that it is NANCY.

HOLLY: Is it?

DOM nods.

DOM: They say that, at the end, your whole life flashes before your eyes. But now it's like her whole life is replaying before me. Edited highlights.

ROSIE: There's teachers up there with her.

BILLY: It's Miss Sparkes and Miss Underwood.

DOM: I am five and Dad's bought a dog for Nancy's 7th birthday. She wants to call him Sandy but I cry so hard that she agrees to call him Alan even thought it's a stupid name for a dog. How could she be so...stupid?

ALEX: The police are there.

NADIA: Where?

ALEX: There. Can you see the reflection of the lights?

DOM: I am seven and she's flashing her torch under my bed to help me feel safe from monsters.

JAMIE: They're helping her.

DOM: I am nine and she's sharing her headphones to drown out our parents arguing before Dad moves out.

BILLY: They're talking to her.

ALEX: What are they saying?

BILLY: I can't hear but she's listening.

DOM: I am ten and I am pretending to hate going to her street dance shows but really I am so proud of her.

ROSIE: There's an ambulance.

DOM: I am 11 and we're in lockdown and we're taking Alan for these really long walks for our mental health.

HOLLY: She looks like she's moving away from the edge.

DOM: It's six or eight months ago and I know something's off with her.

She's having these long naps–some weekends barely getting up at all. Like she's fading away to nothing.

And she getting really skinny.

And she stopped talking to me. She stopped talking to everyone.

But then she's too awake like she's on fire.

Moving too fast.

Scrambling her words as she tries to make sense of her thoughts. And it is like everything has led up to this moment.

The dog naming.

The flashlight.

Shared headphones, dance shows and arguments.

The long lockdown walks.

Have all led to this moment with me stuck in this classroom
And Nancy on the roof.

If she....

I will never get over it.

I feel angry

'Cause how can she do that to herself when she knows that she is so loved? And I get that she can't help it.

That she's clearly not very well and needs some help.

And I should have told someone.

Looked out for her like she's looked out for me.

And if she....

I'll never forgive myself.

HOLLY: Miss has given her her coat.

JAMIE: She must have be freezing up there.

ALEX: Dom. I think it's going to be OK.

JAMIE: They're going down the fire escape.

HOLLY: It's over.

DOM: I need to get to her.

JAMIE goes to unlock the door.

ALEX: I'm coming with you.

JAMIE lets DOM past and ALEX follows.

SCENE 23

ROSIE: That was ...

NADIA: Yeah it was...

ROSIE: You know you can talk to me if you ever needed to ...you know.

NADIA: Thanks.

ROSIE: (*To HOLLY*) You coming?

HOLLY: I'll catch you up.

NADIA and ROSIE leave together.

JAMIE: (*To HOLLY indicating BILLY*) Are they going to be alright?

BILLY: I'm fine. Jamie. Are you going to be alright?

JAMIE: Me? I'm fine. Totally fine.

JAMIE picks up his stuff and leaves.

HOLLY: Do you think Nancy's going to be OK?

BILLY: Yeah. They'll take her to hospital and give her a full assessment. They'll help her. I'm just thinking about Dom.

HOLLY: Yeah.

BILLY: We can keep an eye on him.

HOLLY: Yeah.

BILLY: You alright?

HOLLY: Not really. You?

BILLY: Me neither.

HOLLY: I don't think anyone's completely OK.

BILLY: And that's OK.

HOLLY: Hug?

BILLY: I can offer a friendly handshake.

HOLLY: Nice.

They shake hands.

ALSO AVAILABLE FROM SALAMANDER STREET

All Salamander Street plays can be bought in bulk at a discount for performance or study. Contact info@salamanderstreet.com to enquire about performance liscenses.

HIDDEN by Nina Lemon
ISBN: 9781913630584

A play about self-worth, mental health and self harm. This play, for year 8+ has been developed in consultation with clinicians, those who have recovered from self-harm and leading charities.

LOSING IT by Nina Lemon
ISBN: 9781913630560

This musical play offers year 9+ students a new take on sex education, telling the story of a group of 18 year olds as they look back on their 7 years at secondary school.

COWBOYS AND LESBIANS by Billie Esplen
ISBN: 9781914228902

A queer romantic comedy which examines the intersection between sexuality and fantasy through the eyes of two closeted teenage girls, highlighting just how much the stories we consume affect the ones we tell about ourselves.

BALISONG by Jennifer Adam
ISBN: 9781914228377

Charting the journey of four friends through the final weeks of school. They're facing a dilemma. What should they do now that one of their friends is carrying a knife?

PLACEHOLDER by Catherine Bisset
ISBN: 9781914228919

Profoundly thought-provoking, this solo play about the historical actor-singer of colour known as 'Minette' offers an exploration of the complex racial and social dynamics of what would become the first independent nation in the Caribbean.